GITANJALI

RABINDRANATH TAGORE

GITANJALI

OFFERINGS

of

SONG

and ART

PAINTINGS BY MARK W. McGINNIS

First edition, 2005

This project received support from a Nora Staael Evert Research Award from Northern State University. Printed and bound in China.

ISBN 1-891-640-28-3
Distributed in North America by:
ACC Distribution
1-800-252-5231
www.antiquecollectorsclub.com

ISBN: 81-88204-39-0
Published in South Asia by:
Mapin Publishing
31 Somnath Road, Usmanpura
Ahmedabad, India 380 013
Tel: 91-79-2755 1833 / Fax: 2755 0955
mapin@icenet.net / www.mapinpub.com

For distribution elsewhere in the world, contact:
Floating World Editions
26 Jack Corner Road
Warren, CT 06777 USA
Tel: 860-868-0890
www.floatingworldeditions.com

PUBLISHER'S NOTE

"I have carried the manuscript of these translations about with me for days, reading it in railway trains, or on the top of omnibuses and in restaurants, and I have often had to close it lest some stranger would see how much it moved me."

So wrote the Irish poet W.B. Yeats in his introduction to *Gitanjali* (meaning *Song Offerings*) when it appeared in 1912. The book's author, Bengali poet, novelist, and educator Rabindranath Tagore (1861–1941), is widely considered the greatest figure in modern Indian letters, and won the Nobel Prize for Literature in 1913. Since dozens of editions of *Gitanjali* in many languages have appeared since then, the question of whether another is needed is legitimate; an affirmative answer comes through briefly reconsidering both the author and the work.

Aside from his literary fame, Tagore was lauded as a great reformer and vigorous opponent of English colonialism. (Awarded a knighthood, he surrendered it in 1919 after British troops killed some 400 Indian demonstrators at Amritsar.) Yet although his pacifist views greatly influenced Gandhi and others, he warned often and forcefully about the dangers of adherence to narrow national and group interests, which he rightly foresaw would drag the world toward international conflict. He advocated understanding, tolerance, and restraint, qualities sorely lacking in relations among nations today.

The *Song Offerings* themselves are widely interpreted as evincing a longing for union with the divine, with their primary sources in the teachings of the *Upanishads*. Yet they are all-embracing and ecumenical, attesting to the universal nature of the spiritual search: "When one knows thee, then alien there is none, then no door is shut." Again, they reflect a spirit of forbearance, acceptance, and magnanimity.

So, yes, in these times of political and religious strife we do indeed need to become reacquainted with and re-inspired by this great mind of modern times. It is the publisher's and artist's hope that this modest edition can bring more people to know Tagore and his *Song Offerings,* and perhaps help us both to envision and to create a world that "has not been broken up into fragments / by narrow domestic walls."

ARTIST'S STATEMENT

In the summer of 2001 I began reading the works of Tagore and soon discovered this book. I immediately knew that I needed to drop what I was currently working on and begin a series of paintings inspired by these poems. The book consists of 103 "song offerings"; my project was to create one nine-by-nine-inch painting for each poem. I decided on the small size to harmonize with the very intimate nature of the poetry and to allude to the Indian miniature paintings of past centuries.

To produce the *Gitanjali* project I attempted to submerge myself in Tagore's world. I read material from all areas of his diverse and creative career. The paintings are not meant to be illustrations of the verses but images inspired by the poetry and by my understanding of the creative mind behind them. This understanding is then merged with my own sense of aesthetics, my evolving painting technique, and my interest in Indian Kangra-style paintings of the late eighteenth century. Elements of paintings XVI, XXXII, XXXV, XXXVII, XL, LX, and LXXIV were inspired by the photography of Gerald Cubit in his wonderful book *Wild India.* One of the things that has made this series such a rewarding experience was my determination early in the project to not be locked to one stylistic approach. Instead I allowed each poem to pull me in whatever direction the verses inspired. This led to freedom that I have not experienced in my previous projects and a path that I plan to follow in the future.

What moved me so deeply in Tagore's poetry was the beautiful honesty in his search for the eternal and his striving to find his relationship with the spiritual. On occasion Tagore's connection with his Hindu roots became wonderfully evident in his allusions to traditional devotional imagery. In several paintings I have suggested this with blue-skinned figures that refer to Vishnu and his other manifestations such as Krishna, Rama, and Buddha. But in spite of my interest in Hindu religion and culture what primarily drew me to Tagore's poetry was its universality. I felt that a Jew, a Christian, a Muslim, a follower of nearly any religious tradition, could draw inspiration from Tagore's wisdom and insight.

—Mark W. McGinnis, 2005

GITANJALI

I

Thou hast made me endless, such is thy pleasure.
This frail vessel thou emptiest again and again, and fillest it
    ever with fresh life.
This little flute of a reed thou hast carried over hills and dales,
    and hast breathed through it melodies eternally new.
At the immortal touch of thy hands my little heart loses its
    limits in joy and gives birth to utterance ineffable.
Thy infinite gifts come to me only on these very small hands
    of mine. Ages pass, and still thou pourest, and still
    there is room to fill.

II

When thou commandest me to sing it seems that my heart
would break with pride; and I look to thy face, and
tears come to my eyes.
All that is harsh and dissonant in my life melts into one
sweet harmony—and my adoration spreads wings like
a glad bird on its flight across the sea.
I know thou takest pleasure in my singing. I know that only
as a singer I come before thy presence.
I touch by the edge of the far-spreading wing of my song thy
feet which I could never aspire to reach.
Drunk with the joy of singing I forget myself and call thee
friend who art my lord.

III

I know not how thou singest, my master! I ever listen in
     silent amazement.

The light of thy music illumines the world. The life breath of
     thy music runs from sky to sky. The holy stream of thy
     music breaks through all stony obstacles and rushes on.

My heart longs to join in thy song, but vainly struggles for a
     voice. I would speak, but speech breaks not into song,
     and I cry out baffled. Ah, thou hast made my heart
     captive in the endless meshes of thy music, my master!

IV

Life of my life, I shall ever try to keep my body pure,
      knowing that thy living touch is upon all my limbs.
I shall ever try to keep all untruths out from my thoughts,
      knowing that thou art that truth which has kindled
      the light of reason in my mind.
I shall ever try to drive all evils away from my heart and
      keep my love in flower, knowing that thou hast thy
      seat in the inmost shrine of my heart.
And it shall be my endeavour to reveal thee in my actions,
      knowing it is thy power gives me strength to act.

V

I ask for a moment's indulgence to sit by thy side.

The works that I have in hand I will finish afterwards.

Away from the sight of thy face my heart knows no rest nor
respite, and my work becomes an endless toil in a
shoreless sea of toil.

Today the summer has come at my window with its sighs
and murmurs; and the bees are plying their minstrelsy
at the court of the flowering grove.

Now it is time to sit quiet, face to face with thee, and to sing
dedication of life in this silent and overflowing leisure.

VI

Pluck this little flower and take it, delay not! I fear lest it
     droop and drop into the dust.
I may not find a place in thy garland, but honour it with a
     touch of pain from thy hand and pluck it. I fear lest
     the day end before I am aware, and the time of offering
     go by.
Though its colour be not deep and its smell be faint, use this
     flower in thy service and pluck it while there is time.

VII

My song has put off her adornments.

She has no pride of dress and decoration.

Ornaments would mar our union; they would come
between thee and me; their jingling would drown thy
whispers.

My poet's vanity dies in shame before thy sight.

O master poet, I have sat down at thy feet.

Only let me make my life simple and straight, like a flute of
reed for thee to fill with music.

VIII

The child who is decked with prince's robes and who has
    jewelled chains round his neck loses all pleasure in his
    play; his dress hampers him at every step.
In fear that it may be frayed, or stained with dust he keeps
    himself from the world, and is afraid even to move.
Mother, it is no gain, thy bondage of finery, if it keeps one
    shut off from the healthful dust of the earth, if it rob
    one of the right of entrance to the great fair of
    common human life.

IX

O Fool, try to carry thyself upon thy own shoulders!
O beggar, to come beg at thy own door!
Leave all thy burdens on his hands who can bear all, and
      never look behind in regret.
Thy desire at once puts out the light from the lamp it
      touches with its breath. It is unholy—take not thy
      gifts through its unclean hands.
Accept only what is offered by sacred love.

X

Here is thy footstool and there rest thy feet where live the
poorest, and lowliest, and lost.

When I try to bow to thee, my obeisance cannot reach down
to the depth where thy feet rest among the poorest,
and lowliest, and lost.

Pride can never approach to where thou walkest in the
clothes of the humble among the poorest, and
lowliest, and lost.

My heart can never find its way to where thou keepest
company with the companionless among the poorest,
the lowliest, and the lost.

XI

Leave this chanting and singing and telling of beads!
Whom dost thou worship in this lonely dark corner of a
      temple with doors all shut?
Open thine eyes and see thy God is not before thee!
He is there where the tiller is tilling the hard ground and
      where the pathmaker is breaking stones.
He is with them in sun and in shower, and his garment is
      covered with dust. Put off thy holy mantle and even
      like him come down on the dusty soil!
Deliverance?
Where is this deliverance to be found?
Our master himself has joyfully taken upon him the bonds
      of creation; he is bound with us all forever.
Come out of thy meditations and leave aside thy flowers and
      incense!
What harm is there if thy clothes become tattered and
      stained?
Meet him and stand by him in toil and in sweat of thy brow.

XII

The time that my journey takes is long and the way of it
      long.
I came out on the chariot of the first gleam of light, and
      pursued my voyage through the wildernesses of
      worlds leaving my track on many a star and planet.
It is the most distant course that comes nearest to thyself,
      and that training is the most intricate which leads to
      the utter simplicity of a tune.
The traveler has to knock at every alien door to come to his
      own, and one has to wander through all the outer
      worlds to reach the innermost shrine at the end.
My eyes strayed far and wide before I shut them and said
"Here art thou!"
The question and the cry "Oh, where?" melt into tears of a
      thousand streams and deluge the world with the flood
      of the assurance "I am!"

XIII

The song that I came to sing remains unsung to this day.
I have spent my days in stringing and in unstringing my
      instrument.
The time has not come true, the words have not been rightly
      set; only there is the agony of wishing in my heart.
The blossom has not opened; only the wind is sighing by.
I have not seen his face, nor have I listened to his voice; only
      I have heard his gentle footsteps from the road before
      my house.
The livelong day has passed in spreading his seat on the
      floor; but the lamp has not been lit and I cannot ask
      him into my house.
I live in the hope of meeting with him; but this meeting is
      not yet.

XII

The time that my journey takes is long and the way of it
      long.

I came out on the chariot of the first gleam of light, and
      pursued my voyage through the wildernesses of
      worlds leaving my track on many a star and planet.

It is the most distant course that comes nearest to thyself,
      and that training is the most intricate which leads to
      the utter simplicity of a tune.

The traveler has to knock at every alien door to come to his
      own, and one has to wander through all the outer
      worlds to reach the innermost shrine at the end.

My eyes strayed far and wide before I shut them and said
"Here art thou!"

The question and the cry "Oh, where?" melt into tears of a
      thousand streams and deluge the world with the flood
      of the assurance "I am!"

XIII

The song that I came to sing remains unsung to this day.
I have spent my days in stringing and in unstringing my
    instrument.
The time has not come true, the words have not been rightly
    set; only there is the agony of wishing in my heart.
The blossom has not opened; only the wind is sighing by.
I have not seen his face, nor have I listened to his voice; only
    I have heard his gentle footsteps from the road before
    my house.
The livelong day has passed in spreading his seat on the
    floor; but the lamp has not been lit and I cannot ask
    him into my house.
I live in the hope of meeting with him; but this meeting is
    not yet.

XIV

My desires are many and my cry is pitiful, but ever didst
    thou save me by hard refusals; and this strong mercy
    has been wrought into my life through and through.
Day by day thou art making me worthy of the simple, great
    gifts that thou gavest to me unasked—this sky and the
    light, this body and the life and the mind—saving me
    from perils of overmuch desire.
There are times when I languidly linger and times when I
    awaken and hurry in search of my goal; but cruelly
    thou hidest thyself from before me.
Day by day thou art making me worthy of thy full
    acceptance by refusing me ever and anon, saving me
    from perils of weak, uncertain desire.

XV

I am here to sing thee songs. In this hall of thine I have a
    corner seat.
In thy world I have no work to do; my useless life can only
    break out in tunes without a purpose.
When the hour strikes for thy silent worship at the dark
    temple of midnight, command me, my master, to
    stand before thee to sing.
When in the morning air the golden harp is tuned, honour
    me, commanding my presence.

XVI

I have had my invitation to this world's festival, and thus my
    life has been blessed. My eyes have seen and my ears
    have heard.

It was my part at this feast to play upon my instrument, and
    I have done all I could.

Now, I ask, has the time come at last when I may go in and
    see thy face and offer thee my silent salutation?

XVII

I am only waiting for love to give myself up at last into
    his hands.
That is why it is so late and why I have been guilty of such
    omissions.
They come with their laws and their codes to bind me fast;
    but I evade them ever, for I am only waiting for love to
    give myself up at last into his hands.
People blame me and call me heedless; I doubt not they are
    right in their blame.
The market day is over and work is all done for the busy.
Those who came to call me in vain have gone back in anger.
I am only waiting for love to give myself up at last into
    his hands.

XVIII

Clouds heap upon clouds and it darkens. Ah, love, why dost
  thou let me wait outside at the door all alone?
In the busy moments of the noontide work I am with the
  crowd, but on this dark lonely day it is only for thee
  that I hope.
If thou showest me not thy face, if thou leavest me wholly
  aside, I know not how I am to pass these long, rainy
  hours.
I keep gazing on the far-away gloom of the sky, and my
  heart wanders wailing with the restless wind.

XIX

If thou speakest not I will fill my heart with thy silence and
      endure it.

I will keep still and wait like the night with starry vigil and
      its head bent low with patience.

The morning will surely come, the darkness will vanish, and
      thy voice pour down in golden streams breaking
      through the sky.

Then thy words will take wing in songs from every one of
      my birds' nests, and thy melodies will break forth in
      flowers in all my forest groves.

XX

On the day when the lotus bloomed, alas, my mind was
straying, and I knew it not. My basket was empty and
the flower remained unheeded.
Only now and again a sadness fell upon me, and I started up
from my dream and felt a sweet trace of a strange
fragrance in the south wind.
That vague sweetness made my heart ache with longing and
it seemed to me that is was the eager breath of the
summer seeking for its completion.
I knew not then that it was so near, that it was mine, and
that this perfect sweetness had blossomed in the depth
of my own heart.

XXI

I must launch out my boat. The languid hours pass by on
    the shore—Alas for me!
The spring has done its flowering and taken leave.
And now with the burden of faded futile flowers I wait
    and linger.
The waves have become clamorous, and upon the bank in
    the shady lane the yellow leaves flutter and fall.
What emptiness do you gaze upon!
Do you not feel a thrill passing through the air with the
    notes of the far-away song floating from the
    other shore?

XXII

In the deep shadows of the rainy July, with secret steps, thou
walkest, silent as night, eluding all watchers.

Today the morning has closed its eyes, heedless of the
insistent calls of the loud east wind, and a thick veil
has been drawn over the ever-wakeful blue sky.

The woodlands have hushed their songs, and doors are all
shut at every house. Thou art the solitary wayfarer in
this deserted street.

Oh my only friend, my best beloved, the gates are open in
my house—do not pass by like a dream.

XXIII

Art thou abroad on this stormy night on thy journey of
     love, my friend?
The sky groans like one in despair.
I have no sleep tonight.
Ever and again I open my door and look out on the
     darkness, my friend!
I can see nothing before me.
I wonder where lies thy path!
By what dim shore of the ink-black river, by what far edge of
     the frowning forest, through what mazy depth of
     gloom art thou threading thy course to come to me,
     my friend?

XXIV

If the day is done, if birds sing no more, if the wind has
    flagged tired, then draw the veil of darkness thick
    upon me, even as thou hast wrapt the earth with the
    coverlet of sleep and tenderly closed the petals of the
    drooping lotus at dusk.
From the traveler, whose sack of provisions is empty before
    the voyage is ended, whose garment is torn and dust
    laden, whose strength is exhausted, remove shame
    and poverty, and renew his life like a flower under the
    cover of thy kindly night.

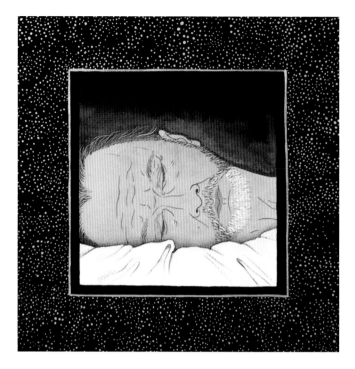

XXV

In the night of weariness let me give myself up to sleep
    without struggle, resting my trust upon thee.
Let me not force my flagging spirit into a poor preparation
    for thy worship.
It is thou who drawest the veil of night upon the tired eyes
    of the day to renew its sight in a fresher gladness of
    awakening.

XXVI

He came and sat by my side but I woke not. What a cursed
      sleep it was, O miserable me!
He came when the night was still; he had his harp in his
      hands, and my dreams became resonant with its
      melodies.
Alas, why are my nights all thus lost?
Ah, why do I ever miss his sight whose breath touches
      my sleep?

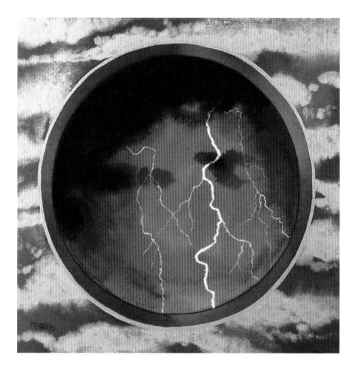

XXVII

Light, oh where is the light?

Kindle it with the burning fire of desire!

There is the lamp but never a flicker of a flame—is such thy
    fate, my heart?

Ah, death were better by far for thee!

Misery knocks at thy door, and her message is that thy lord
    is wakeful, and he calls thee to the love-tryst through
    the darkness of night.

The sky is overcast with clouds and the rain is ceaseless.

I know not what this is that stirs in me—I know not
    its meaning.

A moment's flash of lightning drags down a deeper gloom
    on my sight, and my heart gropes for the path to
    where the music of the night calls me.

Light, oh where is the light! Kindle it with the burning fire
    of desire!

It thunders and the wind rushes screaming through the void.

The night is black as a black stone. Let not the hours pass by
    in the dark.

Kindle the lamp of love with thy life.

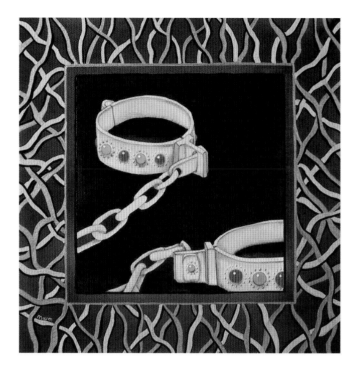

XXVIII

Obstinate are the trammels, but my heart aches when I try
to break them.

Freedom is all I want, but to hope for it I feel ashamed.

I am certain that priceless wealth is in thee, and that thou
art my best friend, but I have not the heart to sweep
away the tinsel that fills my room.

The shroud that covers me is a shroud of dust and death; I
hate it, yet hug it in love.

My debts are large, my failures great, my shame secret and
heavy; yet when I come to ask for my good, I quake in
fear lest my prayer be granted.

XXIX

He whom I enclose with my name is weeping in this dungeon.
I am ever busy building this wall all around; and as this wall
     goes up into the sky day by day I lose sight of my true
     being in its dark shadow.
I take pride in this great wall, and I plaster it with dust and
     sand lest a least hole should be left in this name; and
     for all the care I take I lose sight of my true being.

XXX

I came out alone on my way to my tryst. But who is this
    that follows me in the silent dark?
I move aside to avoid his presence but I escape him not.
He makes the dust rise from the earth with his swagger; he
    adds his loud voice to every word that I utter.
He is my own little self, my lord, he knows no shame; but I
    am ashamed to come to thy door in his company.

XXXI

"Prisoner, tell me, who was it that bound you?"

"It was my master," said the prisoner.

>"I thought I could outdo everybody in the world in
>wealth and power, and I amassed in my own
>treasure-house the money due to my king.

When sleep overcame me I lay upon the bed that was for my
>lord, and on waking up I found I was a prisoner in my
>own treasure-house."

"Prisoner, tell me, who was it that wrought this unbreakable
>chain?"

"It was I," said the prisoner, "who forged this chain very
>carefully. I thought my invincible power would hold
>the world captive leaving me in a freedom undisturbed.

Thus night and day I worked at the chain with huge fires
>and cruel hard strokes.

When at last the work was done and the links were complete
>and unbreakable, I found that it held me in its grip."

XXXII

By all means they try to hold me secure who love me in this
       world. But it is otherwise with thy love which is
       greater than theirs, and thou keepest me free.
Lest I forget them they never venture to leave me alone. But
       day passes by after day and thou art not seen.
If I call not thee in my prayers, if I keep not thee in my
       heart, thy love for me still waits for my love.

XXXIII

When it was day they came into my house and said, "We
    shall only take the smallest room here."
They said, "We shall help you in the worship of your God
    and humbly accept only our own share in his grace";
    and then they took their seat in a corner and they sat
    quiet and meek.
But in the darkness of night I find they break into my sacred
    shrine, strong and turbulent, and snatch with unholy
    greed the offerings from God's altar.

XXXIV

Let only that little be left of me whereby I may name thee
my all.
Let only that little be left of my will whereby I may feel thee
on every side, and come to thee in everything, and
offer to thee my love every moment.
Let only that little be left of me whereby I may never
hide thee.
Let only that little of my fetters be left whereby I am bound
with thy will, and thy purpose is carried out in my
life—and that is the fetter of thy love.

XXXV

Where the mind is without fear and the head is held high;
Where knowledge is free;
Where the world has not been broken up into fragments by
    narrow domestic walls;
Where words come out from the depth of truth;
Where tireless striving stretches its arms towards perfection;
Where the clear stream of reason has not lost its way into
    the dreary desert sand of dead habit;
Where the mind is led forward by thee into ever-widening
    thought and action—
Into that heaven of freedom, my Father, let my country
    awake.

XXXVI

This is my prayer to thee, my lord—strike, strike at the root
    of penury in my heart.
Give me the strength lightly to bear my joys and sorrows.
Give me the strength to make my love fruitful in service.
Give me the strength never to disown the poor or bend my
    knees before insolent might.
Give me the strength to raise my mind high above daily
    trifles.
And give me the strength to surrender my strength to thy
    will with love.

XXXVII

I thought that my voyage had come to its end at the last
     limit of my power—that the path before me was
     closed, that provisions were exhausted and the time
     come to take shelter in a silent obscurity.

But I find that thy will knows no end in me.

And when old words die out on the tongue, new melodies
     break forth from the heart; and where the old tracks
     are lost, new country is revealed with its wonders.

XXXVIII

That I want thee, only thee—let my heart repeat without
    end. All desires that distract me, day and night, are
    false and empty to the core.
As the night keeps hidden in its gloom the petition for light,
    even thus in the depth of my unconsciousness rings
    the cry—"I want thee, only thee."
As the storm still seeks its end in peace when it strikes
    against peace with all its might, even thus my
    rebellion strikes against thy love and still its cry
    is—"I want thee, only thee."

XXXIX

When the heart is hard and parched up, come upon me with
a shower of mercy.

When grace is lost from life, come with a burst of song.

When tumultuous work raises its din on all sides shutting
me out from beyond, come to me, my lord of silence,
with thy peace and rest.

When my beggarly heart sits crouched, shut up in a corner,
break open the door, my king, and come with the
ceremony of a king.

When desire blinds the mind with delusion and dust,
O thou holy one, thou wakeful, come with thy light
and thy thunder.

XL

The rain has held back for days and days, my God, in my
arid heart. The horizon is fiercely naked—not the
thinnest cover of a soft cloud, not the vaguest hint of a
distant cool shower.

Send thy angry storm, dark with death, if it is thy wish,
and with lashes of lightning startle the sky from end
to end.

But call back, my lord, call back this pervading silent heat,
still and keen and cruel, burning the heart with dire
despair.

Let the cloud of grace bend low from above like the tearful
look of the mother on the day of the father's wrath.

XLI

Where dost thou stand behind them all, my lover, hiding
thyself in the shadows?
They push thee and pass thee by on the dusty road, taking
thee for naught.
I wait here weary hours spreading my offerings for thee,
while passers-by come and take my flowers, one by
one, and my basket is nearly empty.
The morning time is past, and the noon.
In the shade of evening my eyes are drowsy with sleep.
Men going home glance at me and smile and fill me
with shame.
I sit like a beggar maid, drawing my skirt over my face, and
when they ask me, what it is I want, I drop my eyes
and answer them not.
Oh, how, indeed, could I tell them that for thee I wait, and
that thou hast promised to come.
How could I utter for shame that I keep for my dowry this
poverty.

Ah, I hug this pride in the secret of my heart.
I sit on the grass and gaze upon the sky and dream of the
  sudden splendour of thy coming—all the lights
  ablaze, golden pennons flying over thy car, and they at
  the roadside standing agape, when they see thee come
  down from thy seat to raise me from the dust, and set
  at thy side this ragged beggar girl a-tremble with
  shame and pride, like a creeper in a summer breeze.
But time glides on and still no sound of the wheels of thy
  chariot. Many a procession passes by with noise
  and shouts and glamour of glory. Is it only thou
  who wouldst stand in the shadow silent and behind
  them all?
And only I who would wait and weep and wear out my
  heart in vain longing?

XLII

Early in the day it was whispered that we should sail in a
    boat, only thou and I, and never a soul in the world
    would know of this our pilgrimage to no country and
    to no end.
In that shoreless ocean, at thy silently listening smile my
    songs would swell in melodies, free as waves, free from
    all bondage of words.
Is the time not come yet?
Are there works still to do?
Lo, the evening has come down upon the shore and in the
    fading light the seabirds come flying to their nests.
Who knows when the chains will be off, and the boat, like
    the last glimmer of sunset, vanish into the night?

XLIII

The day was when I did not keep myself in readiness for
thee; and entering my heart unbidden even as one of
the common crowd, unknown to me, my king, thou
didst press the signet of eternity upon many a fleeting
moment of my life.

And today when by chance I light upon them and see thy
signature, I find they have lain scattered in the dust
mixed with the memory of joys and sorrows of my
trivial days forgotten.

Thou didst not turn in contempt from my childish play
among dust, and the steps that I heard in my
playroom are the same that are echoing from star
to star.

XLII

Early in the day it was whispered that we should sail in a
    boat, only thou and I, and never a soul in the world
    would know of this our pilgrimage to no country and
    to no end.
In that shoreless ocean, at thy silently listening smile my
    songs would swell in melodies, free as waves, free from
    all bondage of words.
Is the time not come yet?
Are there works still to do?
Lo, the evening has come down upon the shore and in the
    fading light the seabirds come flying to their nests.
Who knows when the chains will be off, and the boat, like
    the last glimmer of sunset, vanish into the night?

XLIII

The day was when I did not keep myself in readiness for
    thee; and entering my heart unbidden even as one of
    the common crowd, unknown to me, my king, thou
    didst press the signet of eternity upon many a fleeting
    moment of my life.
And today when by chance I light upon them and see thy
    signature, I find they have lain scattered in the dust
    mixed with the memory of joys and sorrows of my
    trivial days forgotten.
Thou didst not turn in contempt from my childish play
    among dust, and the steps that I heard in my
    playroom are the same that are echoing from star
    to star.

XLIV

This is my delight, thus to wait and watch at the wayside
 where shadow chases light and the rain comes in the
 wake of the summer.
Messengers, with tidings from unknown skies, greet me and
 speed along the road.
My heart is glad within, and the breath of the passing breeze
 is sweet.
From dawn till dusk I sit here before my door, and I know
 that of a sudden the happy moment will arrive when I
 shall see.
In the meanwhile I smile and I sing all alone.
In the meanwhile the air is filling with the perfume of
 promise.

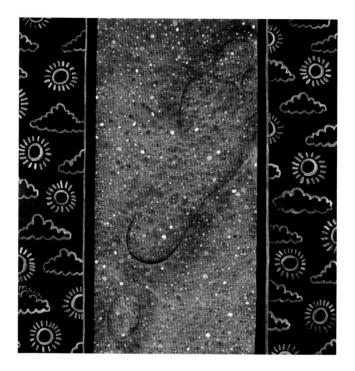

XLV

Have you not heard his silent steps?
He comes, comes, ever comes.
Every moment and every age, every day and every night he
    comes, comes, ever comes.
Many a song have I sung in many a mood of mind, but all
    their notes have always proclaimed, "He comes,
    comes, ever comes."
In the fragrant days of sunny April through the forest path
    he comes, comes, ever comes.
In the rainy gloom of July nights on the thundering chariot
    of clouds he comes, comes, ever comes.
In sorrow after sorrow it is his steps that press upon my
    heart, and it is the golden touch of his feet that makes
    my joy to shine.

XLVI

I know not from what distant time thou art ever coming
     nearer to meet me.
Thy sun and stars can never keep thee hidden from me
     for aye.
In many a morning and eve thy footsteps have been heard
     and thy messenger has come within my heart and
     called me in secret.
I know not only why today my life is all astir, and a feeling
     of tremulous joy is passing through my heart.
It is as if the time were come to wind up my work, and I feel
     in the air a faint smell of thy sweet presence.

XLVII

The night is nearly spent waiting for him in vain.
I fear lest in the morning he suddenly come to my door
     when I have fallen asleep wearied out.
Oh friends, leave the way open to him—forbid him not.
If the sounds of his steps does not wake me, do not try to
     rouse me, I pray.
I wish not to be called from my sleep by the clamorous
     choir of birds, by the riot of wind at the festival of
     morning light.
Let me sleep undisturbed even if my lord comes of a sudden
     to my door.
Ah, my sleep, precious sleep, which only waits for his touch
     to vanish.
Ah, my closed eyes that would open their lids only to the
     light of his smile when he stands before me like a
     dream emerging from darkness of sleep.
Let him appear before my sight as the first of all lights and
     all forms.
The first thrill of joy to my awakened soul let it come from
     his glance.
And let my return to myself be immediate return to him.

XLVIII

The morning sea of silence broke into ripples of bird songs;
    and the flowers were all merry by the roadside; and
    the wealth of gold was scattered through the rift of
    the clouds while we busily went on our way and paid
    no heed.

We sang no glad songs nor played; we went not to the village
    for barter; we spoke not a word nor smiled; we
    lingered not on the way.

We quickened our pace more and more as the time sped by.

The sun rose to the mid sky and doves cooed in the shade.

Withered leaves danced and whirled in the hot air of noon.

The shepherd boy drowsed and dreamed in the shadow of
    the banyan tree, and I laid myself down by the water
    and stretched my tired limbs on the grass.

My companions laughed at me in scorn; they held their
    heads high and hurried on; they never looked back
    nor rested; they vanished in the distant blue haze.

They crossed many meadows and hills, and passed through
    strange, far-away countries.

All honour to you, heroic host of the interminable path!

Mockery and reproach pricked me to rise, but found no
    response in me.

I gave myself up for lost in the depth of a glad humiliation—
    in the shadow of a dim delight.

The repose of the sun-embroidered green gloom slowly
    spread over my heart.

I forgot for what I had traveled, and I surrendered my mind
    without struggle to the maze of shadows and songs.

At last, when I woke from my slumber and opened my eyes,
    I saw thee standing by me, flooding my sleep with thy
    smile.

How I had feared that the path was long and wearisome, and
    the struggle to reach thee was hard!

XLIX

You came down from your throne and stood at my
      cottage door.
I was singing all alone in a corner, and the melody
      caught your ear. You came down and stood at
      my cottage door.
Masters are many in your hall, and songs are sung there
      at all hours. But the simple carol of this novice struck
      at your love.
One plaintive little strain mingled with the great music
      of the world, and with a flower for a prize you came
      down and stopped at my cottage door.

L

I had gone a-begging from door to door in the village path,
        when thy golden chariot appeared in the distance like
        a gorgeous dream and I wondered who was this King
        of all kings!
My hopes rose high and methought my evil days were at an
        end, and I stood waiting for alms to be given unasked
        and for wealth scattered on all sides in the dust.
The chariot stopped where I stood.
Thy glance fell on me and thou camest down with a smile.
I felt that the luck of my life had come at last.
Then of a sudden thou didst hold out thy right hand and say
        "What hast thou to give to me?"
Ah, what a kingly jest was it to open thy palm to a beggar
        to beg!

I was confused and stood undecided, and then from my
      wallet I slowly took out the least little grain of corn
      and gave it to thee.

But how great my surprise when at the day's end I emptied
      my bag on the floor to find a least little grain of gold
      among the poor heap.

I bitterly wept and wished that I had had the heart to give
      thee my all.

LI

The night darkened.

Our day's works had been done.

We thought that the last guest had arrived for the night and
        the doors in the village were all shut.

Only some said the king was to come.

We laughed and said, "No, it cannot be!"

It seemed there were knocks at the door and we said it was
        nothing but the wind.

We put out the lamps and lay down to sleep.

        Only some said, "It is the messenger!" We laughed and
        said "No, it must be the wind!"

There came a sound in the dead of the night.

We sleepily thought it was the distant thunder.

The earth shook, the walls rocked, and it troubled us in our
        sleep.

Only some said it was the sound of wheels.

We said in a drowsy murmur, "No, it must be the rumbling
of clouds!"

The night was still dark when the drum sounded.

The voice came "Wake up! delay not!"

We pressed our hands on our hearts and shuddered with fear.

Some said, "Lo, there is the king's flag!"

We stood up on our feet and cried "There is no time for delay!"

The king has come—but where are lights, where are wreaths?

Where is the throne to seat him?

Oh, shame!

Oh utter shame!

Where is the hall, the decorations? Someone has said, "Vain
is this cry! Greet him with empty hands, lead him into
thy rooms all bare!"

Open the doors, let the conch-shells be sounded!

In the depth of the night has come the king of our dark,
dreary house.

The thunder roars in the sky.

The darkness shudders with lightning.

Bring out thy tattered piece of mat and spread it in the
courtyard.

With the storm has come of a sudden our king of the
fearful night.

LII

I thought I should ask of thee—but I dared not——the rose
   wreath thou hadst on thy neck.

Thus I waited for the morning, when thou didst depart, to
   find a few fragments on the bed.

And like a beggar I searched in the dawn only for a stray
   petal or two.

Ah me, what is it I find?

What token left of thy love?

It is no flower, no spices, no vase of perfumed water.

It is thy mighty sword, flashing as a flame, heavy as a bolt of
   thunder.

The young light of morning comes through the window
   and spread itself upon thy bed.

The morning bird twitters and asks, "Woman, what hast
   thou got?"

No, it is no flower, nor spices, nor vase of perfumed water—
    it is thy dreadful sword.
I sit and muse in wonder, what gift is this of thine.
I can find no place to hide it. I am ashamed to wear it, frail as
    I am, and it hurts me when press it to my bosom.
Yet shall I bear in my heart this honour of the burden of
    pain, this gift of thine.
From now there shall be no fear left for me in this world,
and thou shalt be victorious in all my strife.
Thou hast left death for my companion and I shall crown
    him with my life.
Thy sword is with me to cut asunder my bonds, and there
    shall be no fear left for me in the world.
From now I leave off all petty decorations.
Lord of my heart, no more shall there be for me waiting and
    weeping in corners, no more coyness and sweetness of
    demeanour.
Thou hast given me thy sword for adornment.
No more doll's decorations for me!

LIII

Beautiful is thy wristlet, decked with stars and cunningly
    wrought in myriad-coloured jewels.
But more beautiful to me thy sword with its curve of
    lightning like the outspread wings of the divine bird of
    Vishnu, perfectly poised in the angry red light of the
    sunset.
It quivers like the one last response of life in ecstasy of pain
    at the final stroke of death; it shines like the pure
    flame of being burning up earthly sense with one
    fierce flash.
Beautiful is thy wristlet, decked with starry gems; but thy
    sword, O lord of thunder, is wrought with uttermost
    beauty, terrible to behold or think of.

LIV

I asked nothing from thee; I uttered not my name to
    thine ear.
When thou took'st thy leave I stood silent.
I was alone by the well where the shadow of the tree fell
    aslant, and the women had gone home with their
    brown earthen pitchers full to the brim.
They called me and shouted, "Come with us, the morning is
    wearing on to noon."
But I languidly lingered awhile lost in the midst of vague
    musings.
I heard not thy steps as thou camest.
Thine eyes were sad when they fell on me; thy voice was
    tired as thou spokest low—"Ah, I am a thirsty traveler."
I started up from my day-dreams and poured water from my
    jar on thy joined palms.
The leaves rustled overhead; the cuckoo sang from the
    unseen dark, and perfume of babla flowers came from
    the bend of the road.
I stood speechless with shame when my name thou didst ask.
Indeed, what had I done for thee to keep me in remembrance?
But the memory that I could give water to thee to allay thy
    thirst will cling to my heart and enfold it in sweetness.
The morning hour is late, the bird sings in weary notes, neem
    leaves rustle overhead and I sit and think and think.

LV

Languor is upon your heart and the slumber is still on your
   eyes.
Has not the word come to you that the flower is reigning in
   splendour among thorns?
Wake, oh awaken! Let not the time pass in vain!
At the end of the stony path, in the country of virgin
   solitude, my friend is sitting all alone.
Deceive him not. Wake, oh awaken!
What if the sky pants and trembles with the heat of the
   midday sun—what if the burning sand spreads its
   mantle of thirst—
Is there no joy in the deep of your heart?
At every footfall of yours, will not the harp of the road
   break out in sweet music of pain?

LVI

Thus it is that thy joy in me is so full. Thus it is that thou
    hast come down to me. O thou lord of all heavens,
    where would be thy love if I were not?

Thou hast taken me as thy partner of all this wealth. In my
    heart is the endless play of thy delight. In my life thy
    will is ever taking shape.

And for this, thou who art the King of kings hast decked
    thyself in beauty to captivate my heart. And for this thy
    love loses itself in the love of thy lover, and there art
    thou seen in the perfect union of two.

LVII

Light, my light, the world-filling light, the eye-kissing light,
  heart-sweetening light!
Ah, the light dances, my darling, at the centre of my life;
  the light strikes, my darling, the chords of my love; the
  sky opens, the wind runs wild, laughter passes over
  the earth.
The butterflies spread their sails on the sea of light. Lilies and
  jasmines surge up on the crest of the waves of light.
The light is shattered into gold on every cloud, my darling,
  and it scatters gems in profusion.
Mirth spreads from leaf to leaf, my darling, and gladness
  without measure. The heaven's river has drowned its
  banks and the flood of joy is abroad.

LVIII

Let all the strains of joy mingle in my last song—the joy
    that makes the earth flow over in the riotous excess of
    the grass, the joy that sets the twin brothers, life and
    death, dancing over the wide world, the joy that sweeps
    in with the tempest, shaking and waking all life with
    laughter, the joy that sits still with its tears on the open
    red lotus of pain, and the joy that throws everything it
    has upon the dust, and knows not a word.

LIX

Yes, I know, this is nothing but thy love, O beloved of my
    heart—this golden light that dances upon the leaves,
    these idle clouds sailing across the sky, this passing
    breeze leaving its coolness upon my forehead.
The morning light has flooded my eyes—this is thy message
    to my heart. Thy face is bent from above, thy eyes look
    down on my eyes, and my heart has touched thy feet.

LX

On the seashore of endless worlds children meet.
    The infinite sky is motionless overhead and the restless
    water is boisterous. On the seashore of endless worlds
    the children meet with shouts and dances.
They build their houses with sand and they play with empty
    shells. With withered leaves they weave their boats and
    smilingly float them on the vast deep. Children have
    their play on the seashore of worlds.
They know not how to swim, they know not how to cast
    nets. Pearl fishers dive for pearls, merchants sail in their
    ships, while children gather pebbles and scatter them
    again. They seek not for hidden treasures, they know
    not how to cast nets.
The sea surges up with laughter and pale gleams the smile of
    the sea beach. Death-dealing waves sing meaningless
    ballads to the children, even like a mother while

rocking her baby's cradle. The sea plays with children, and pale gleams the smile of the sea beach.

On the seashore of endless worlds children meet. Tempest roams in the pathless sky, ships get wrecked in the trackless water, death is abroad and children play.

On the seashore of endless worlds is the great meeting of children.

LXI

The sleep that flits on baby's eyes—does anybody know
from where it comes? Yes, there is a rumour that it has
its dwelling where, in the fairy village among shadows
of the forest dimly lit with glow-worms, there hang two
timid buds of enchantment. From there it comes to kiss
baby's eyes.

The smile that flickers on baby's lips when he sleeps—does
anybody know where it was born? Yes, there is a rumour
that a young pale beam of a crescent moon touched the
edge of a vanishing autumn cloud, and there the smile
was first born in the dream of a dew-washed morning—
the smile that flickers on baby's lips when he sleeps.

The sweet, soft freshness that blooms on baby's limbs—does
anybody know where it was hidden so long? Yes, when
the mother was a young girl it lay pervading her heart
in tender and silent mystery of love—the sweet, soft
freshness that has bloomed on baby's limbs.

LXII

When I bring to you coloured toys, my child, I understand
 why there is such a play of colours on clouds, on water,
 and why flowers are painted in tints—when I give
 coloured toys to you, my child.

When I sing to make you dance I truly now why there is
 music in leaves, and why waves send their chorus of
 voices to the heart of the listening earth—when I sing
 to make you dance.

When I bring sweet things to your greedy hands I know why
 there is honey in the cup of the flowers and why fruits
 are secretly filled with sweet juice—when I bring sweet
 things to your greedy hands.

When I kiss your face to make you smile, my darling,
 I surely understand what pleasure streams from the sky
 in morning light, and what delight that is which the
 summer breeze brings to my body—when I kiss you to
 make you smile.

LXIII

Thou hast made me known to friends whom I knew not.
Thou hast given me seats in homes not my own.
Thou hast brought the distant near and made a brother
of the stranger.
I am uneasy at heart when I have to leave my accustomed
shelter; I forget that there abides the old in the new, and
that there also thou abidest.
Through birth and death, in this world or in others,
wherever thou leadest me it is thou, the same, the one
companion of my endless life who ever linkest my heart
with bonds of joy to the unfamiliar.
When one knows thee, then alien there is none, then no
door is shut. Oh, grant me my prayer that I may never
lose the bliss of the touch of the one in the play of
the many.

LXIV

On the slope of the desolate river among tall grasses I asked
her, "Maiden, where do you go shading your lamp with
your mantle? My house is all dark and lonesome—lend
me your light!" She raised her dark eyes for a moment
and looked at my face through the dusk. "I have come
to the river," she said, "to float my lamp on the stream
when the daylight wanes in the west." I stood alone
among tall grasses and watched the timid flame of her
lamp uselessly drifting in the tide.

In the silence of gathering night I asked her, "Maiden, your
lights are all lit—then where do you go with your
lamp? My house is all dark and lonesome—lend me
your light." She raised her dark eyes on my face and
stood for a moment doubtful. "I have come," she said at
last, "to dedicate my lamp to the sky." I stood and
watched her light uselessly burning in the void.

In the moonless gloom of midnight I ask her, "Maiden, what
is your quest, holding the lamp near your heart?
My house is all dark and lonesome—lend me your
light." She stopped for a minute and thought and gazed
at my face in the dark. "I have brought my light," she
said, "to join the carnival of lamps." I stood and watched
her little lamp uselessly lost among lights.

LXV

What divine drink wouldst thou have, my God, from this
overflowing cup of my life?

My poet, is it thy delight to see thy creation through my
eyes and to stand at the portals of my ears silently to
listen to thine own eternal harmony?

Thy world is weaving words in my mind and thy joy is
adding music to them. Thou givest thyself to me in love
and then feelest thine own entire sweetness in me.

LXVI

She who ever had remained in the depth of my being, in the
    twilight of gleams and of glimpses; she who never
    opened her veils in the morning light, will be my last
    gift to thee, my God, folded in my final song.
Words have wooed yet failed to win her; persuasion has
    stretched to her its eager arms in vain.
I have roamed from country to country keeping her in the
    core of my heart, and around her have risen and fallen
    the growth and decay of my life.
Over my thoughts and actions, my slumbers and dreams,
    she reigned yet dwelled alone and apart.
Many a man knocked at my door and asked for her and
    turned away in despair.
There was none in the world who ever saw her face to face,
    and she remained in her loneliness waiting for thy
    recognition.

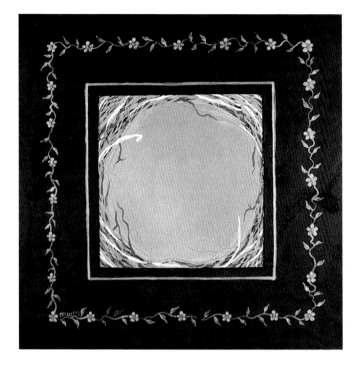

LXVII

Thou art the sky and thou art the nest as well.

O thou beautiful, there in the nest is thy love that encloses
the soul with colours and sounds and odours.

There comes the morning with the golden basket in her
right hand bearing the wreath of beauty, silently to
crown the earth.

And there comes the evening over the lonely meadows
deserted by herds, through trackless paths, carrying
cool draughts of peace in her golden pitcher from the
western ocean of rest.

But there, where spreads the infinite sky for the soul to take
her flight in, reigns the stainless white radiance. There is
no day nor night, nor form nor colour, and never,
never a word.

LXVIII

Thy sunbeam comes upon this earth of mine with arms
    outstretched and stands at my door the livelong day to
    carry back to thy feet clouds made of my tears and sighs
    and songs.
With fond delight thou wrappest about thy starry breast
    that mantle of misty cloud, turning it into numberless
    shapes and folds and colouring it with hues everchanging.
It is so light and so fleeting, tender and tearful and dark, that
    is why thou lovest it, O thou spotless and serene.
    And that is why it may cover thy awful white light with
    its pathetic shadows.

LXIX

The same stream of life that runs through my veins night
and day runs through the world and dances in
rhythmic measures.

It is the same life that shoots in joy through the dust of the
earth in numberless blades of grass and breaks into
tumultuous waves of leaves and flowers.

It is the same life that is rocked in the ocean-cradle of birth
and of death, in ebb and in flow.

I feel my limbs are made glorious by the touch of this world
of life. And my pride is from the life-throb of ages
dancing in my blood this moment.

LXX

Is it beyond thee to be glad with the gladness of this rhythm?
to be tossed and lost and broken in the whirl of this
fearful joy?
All things rush on, they stop not, they look not behind,
no power can hold them back, they rush on.
Keeping steps with that restless, rapid music, seasons come
dancing and pass away—colours, tunes, and perfumes
pour in endless cascades in the abounding joy that
scatters and gives up and dies every moment.

LXXI

That I should make much of myself and turn it on all sides,
thus casting coloured shadows on thy radiance—such is
thy maya.

Thou settest a barrier in thine own being and then callest
thy severed self in myriad notes. This thy self-separation
has taken body in me.

The poignant song is echoed through all the sky in
many-coloured tears and smiles, alarms and hopes;
waves rise up and sink again, dreams break and form.
In me is thy own defeat of self.

This screen that thou hast raised is painted with
innumerable figures with the brush of the night and
the day. Behind it thy seat is woven in wondrous
mysteries of curves, casting away all barren lines of
straightness.

The great pageant of thee and me has overspread the sky.
With the tune of thee and me all the air is vibrant, and
all ages pass with the hiding and seeking of thee and me.

LXXII

He it is, the innermost one, who awakens my being with his
    deep hidden touches.

He it is who puts his enchantment upon these eyes and
    joyfully plays on the chords of my heart in varied
    cadence of pleasure and pain.

He it is who weaves the web of this maya in evanescent hues
    of gold and silver, blue and green, and lets peep out
    through the folds his feet, at whose touch I forget myself.

Days come and ages pass, and it is ever he who moves my
    heart in many a name, in many a guise, in many a
    rapture of joy and of sorrow.

LXXIII

Deliverance is not for me in renunciation. I feel the embrace
of freedom in a thousand bonds of delight.

Thou ever pourest for me the fresh draught of thy wine of
various colours and fragrance, filling this earthen vessel
to the brim.

My world will light its hundred different lamps with thy
flame and place them before the altar of thy temple.

No, I will never shut the doors of my senses. The delights of
sight and hearing and touch will bear thy delight.

Yes, all my illusions will burn into illumination of joy, and
all my desires ripen into fruits of love.

LXXIV

The day is no more, the shadow is upon the earth. It is time
    that I go to the stream to fill my pitcher.
The evening air is eager with the sad music of the water.
    Ah, it calls me out into the dusk. In the lonely lane
    there is no passer-by, the wind is up, the ripples are
    rampant in the river.
I know not if I shall come back home. I know not whom I
    shall chance to meet. There at the fording in the little
    boat the unknown man plays upon his lute.

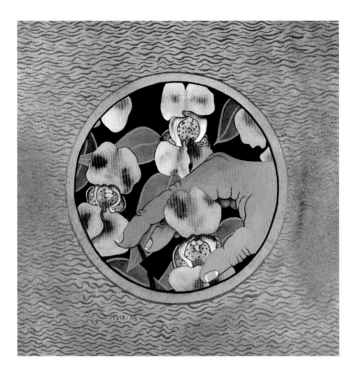

LXXV

Thy gifts to us mortals fulfill all our needs and yet run back
    to thee undiminished.

The river has its everyday work to do and hastens through
    fields and hamlets; yet its incessant stream winds
    towards the washing of thy feet.

The flower sweetens the air with its perfume; yet its last
    service is to offer itself to thee.

Thy worship does not impoverish the world.

From the words of the poet men take what meanings please
    them; yet their last meaning points to thee.

LXXVI

Day after day, O lord of my life, shall I stand before thee face
to face. With folded hands, O lord of all worlds, shall I
stand before thee face to face.

Under thy great sky in solitude and silence, with humble
heart shall I stand before thee face to face.

In this laborious world of thine, tumultuous with toil and
with struggle, among hurrying crowds shall I stand
before thee face to face.

And when my work shall be done in this world, O King of
kings, alone and speechless shall I stand before thee
face to face.

LXXVII

I know thee as my God and stand apart—I do not know
    thee as my own and come closer. I know thee as my
    father and bow before thy feet—I do not grasp thy hand
    as my friend's.

I stand not where thou comest down and ownest thyself as
    mine, there to clasp thee to my heart and take thee as
    my comrade.

Thou art the Brother amongst my brothers, but I heed them
    not, I divide not my earnings with them, thus sharing
    my all with thee.

In pleasure and in pain I stand not by the side of men, and
    thus stand by thee. I shrink to give up my life, and thus
    do not plunge into the great waters of life.

LXXVIII

When the creation was new and all the stars shone in
their first splendour, the gods held their assembly in
the sky and sang "Oh, the picture of perfection!
the joy unalloyed!"

But one cried of a sudden—"It seems that somewhere there
is a break in the chain of light and one of the stars has
been lost."

The golden string of their harp snapped, their song stopped,
and they cried in dismay—"Yes, that lost star was the
best, she was the glory of all heavens!"

From that day the search is unceasing for her, and the cry
goes on from one to the other that in her the world has
lost its one joy!

Only in the deepest silence of night the stars smile and
whisper among themselves—"Vain is this seeking!
Unbroken perfection is over all!"

LXXIX

If it is not my portion to meet thee in this life then let me
ever feel that I have missed thy sight—let me not forget
for a moment, let me carry the pangs of this sorrow in
my dreams and in my wakeful hours.

As my days pass in the crowded market of this world and my
hands grow full with the daily profits, let me ever feel
that I have gained nothing—let me not forget for a
moment, let me carry the pangs of this sorrow in my
dreams and in my wakeful hours.

When I sit by the roadside, tired and panting, when I spread
my bed low in the dust, let me ever feel that the long
journey is still before me—let me not forget a moment,
let me carry the pangs of this sorrow in my dreams and
in my wakeful hours.

When my rooms have been decked out and the flutes sound
and the laughter there is loud, let me ever feel that I
have not invited thee to my house—let me not forget
for a moment, let me carry the pangs of this sorrow in
my dreams and in my wakeful hours.

LXXX

I am like a remnant of a cloud of autumn uselessly roaming
    in the sky, O my sun ever-glorious! Thy touch has not
    yet melted my vapour, making me one with thy light,
    and thus I count months and years separated from thee.

If this be thy wish and if this be thy play, then take this
    fleeting emptiness of mine, paint it with colours, gild it
    with gold, float it on the wanton wind and spread it in
    varied wonders.

And again when it shall be thy wish to end this play at night,
    I shall melt and vanish away in the dark, or it may be in
    a smile of the white morning, in a coolness of purity
    transparent.

LXXXI

On many an idle day have I grieved over lost time. But it is
    never lost, my lord. Thou hast taken every moment of
    my life in thine own hands.
Hidden in the heart of things thou art nourishing seeds into
    sprouts, buds into blossoms, and ripening flowers into
    fruitfulness.
I was tired and sleeping on my idle bed and imagined all
    work had ceased. In the morning I woke up and found
    my garden full with wonders of flowers.

LXXXII

Time is endless in thy hands, my lord. There is none to
count thy minutes.
Days and nights pass and ages bloom and fade like flowers.
Thou knowest how to wait.
Thy centuries follow each other perfecting a small wild flower.
We have no time to lose, and having no time we must
scramble for a chances. We are too poor to be late.
And thus it is that time goes by while I give it to every
querulous man who claims it, and thine altar is empty
of all offerings to the last.
At the end of the day I hasten in fear lest thy gate to be shut;
but I find that yet there is time.

LXXXIII

Mother, I shall weave a chain of pearls for thy neck with
my tears of sorrow.

The stars have wrought their anklets of light to deck thy
feet, but mine will hang upon thy breast.

Wealth and fame come from thee and it is for thee to give
or to withhold them. But this my sorrow is absolutely
mine own, and when I bring it to thee as my offering
thou rewardest me with thy grace.

LXXXIV

It is the pang of separation that spreads throughout the
world and gives birth to shapes innumerable in the
infinite sky.

It is this sorrow of separation that gazes in silence all nights
from star to star and becomes lyric among rustling
leaves in rainy darkness of July.

It is this overspreading pain that deepens into loves and
desires, into sufferings and joy in human homes; and
this it is that ever melts and flows in songs through
my poet's heart.

LXXXV

When the warriors came out first from their master's hall,
    where had they hid their power? Where were their
    armour and their arms?

They looked poor and helpless, and the arrows were
    showered upon them on the day they came out from
    their master's hall.

When the warriors marched back again to their master's hall
    where did they hide their power?

They had dropped the sword and dropped the bow and the
    arrow; peace was on their foreheads, and they had left
    the fruits of their life behind them on the day they
    marched back again to their master's hall.

LXXXVI

Death, thy servant, is at my door. He has crossed the
    unknown sea and brought thy call to my home.
The night is dark and my heart is fearful—yet I will take up
    the lamp, open my gates and bow to him my welcome.
    It is thy messenger who stands at my door.
I will worship him placing at his feet the treasure of my heart.
He will go back with his errand done, leaving a dark shadow
    on my morning; and in my desolate home only my
    forlorn self will remain as my last offering to thee.

LXXXVII

In desperate hope I go and search for her in all the corners
of my room; I find her not.

My house is small and what once has gone from it can never
be regained.

But infinite is thy mansion, my lord, and seeking her I have
to come to thy door.

I stand under the golden canopy of thine evening sky and I
lift my eager eyes to thy face.

I have come to the brink of eternity from which nothing
can vanish—no hope, no happiness, no vision of a face
seen through tears.

Oh, dip my emptied life into that ocean, plunge it into the
deepest fullness. Let me for once feel that lost sweet
touch in the allness of the universe.

LXXXVIII

Deity of the ruined temple! The broken strings of Vina
sing no more your praise. The bells in the evening
proclaim not your time of worship. The air is still and
silent about you.

In your desolate dwelling comes the vagrant spring breeze.
It brings the tidings of flowers—the flowers that for
your worship are offered no more.

Your worshipper of old wanders ever longing for favour still
refused. In the eventide, when fires and shadows mingle
with the gloom of dust, he wearily comes back to the
ruined temple with hunger in his heart.

Many a festival day comes to you in silence, deity of the
ruined temple. Many a night of worship goes away with
lamp unlit.

Many new images are built by masters of cunning art and
carried to the holy stream of oblivion when their time
is come.

Only the deity of the ruined temple remains unworshipped
in deathless neglect.

LXXXIX

No more noisy, loud words from me—such is my master's
 will. Henceforth I deal in whispers. The speech of my
 heart will be carried on in murmurings of a song.

Men hasten to the King's market. All the buyers and sellers
 are there. But I have my untimely leave in the middle
 of the day, in the thick of work.

Let then the flowers come out in my garden, though it is
 not their time; and let the midday bees strike up their
 lazy hum.

Full many an hour have I spent in the strife of the good and
 the evil, but now it is the pleasure of my playmate of the
 empty days to draw my heart on to him; and I know
 not why is this sudden call to what useless inconsequence!

XC

On the day when death will knock at thy door what wilt
    thou offer to him?
Oh, I will set before my guest the full vessel of my life—
    I will never let him go with empty hands.
All the sweet vintage of all my autumn days and summer
    nights, all the earnings and gleanings of my busy life
    will I place before him at the close of my days when
    death will knock at my door.

XCI

O thou the last fulfillment of life, Death, my death, come
and whisper to me!
Day after day I have kept watch for thee; for thee have I
borne the joys and pangs of life.
All that I am, that I have, that I hope and all my love
have ever flowed towards thee in depth of secrecy.
One final glance from thine eyes and my life will be
ever thine own.
The flowers have been woven and the garland is ready
for the bridegroom. After the wedding the bride shall
leave her home and meet her lord alone in the solitude
of night.

XCII

I know that the day will come when my sight of this earth
    shall be lost, and life will take its leave in silence,
    drawing the last curtain over my eyes.
Yet stars will watch at night, and morning rise as before,
    and hours heave like sea waves casting up pleasures
    and pains.
When I think of this end of my moments, the barrier of the
    moments breaks and I see by the light of death thy
    world with its careless treasures. Rare is its lowliest seat,
    rare is its meanest of lives.
Things that I longed for in vain and things that I got—
    let them pass. Let me but truly possess the things that
    I ever spurned and overlooked.

XCIII

I have got my leave. Bid me farewell, my brothers! I bow to
you all and take my departure.

Here I give back the keys of my door—and I give up all claims
to my house. I only ask for last kind words from you.

We were neighbours for long, but I received more than I
could give. Now the day has dawned and the lamp that
lit my dark corner is out. A summons has come and I
am ready for my journey.

XCIV

At this time of my parting, wish me good luck, my friends!
    The sky is flushed with the dawn and my path lies
    beautiful.
Ask not what I have with me to take there. I start on my
    journey with empty hands and expectant heart.
I shall put on my wedding garland. Mine is not the
    red-brown dress of the traveler, and though there are
    dangers on the way I have no fear in mind.
The evening star will come out when my voyage is done
    and the plaintive notes of the twilight melodies be
    struck up from the King's gateway.

XCV

I was not aware of the moment when I first crossed the
     threshold of this life.
What was the power that made me open out into this vast
     mystery like a bud in the forest at midnight!
When in the morning I looked upon the light I felt in a
     moment that I was no stranger in this world, that the
     inscrutable without name and form had taken me in its
     arms in the form of my own mother.
Even so, in death the same unknown will appear as ever
     known to me. And because I love this life, I know I shall
     love death as well.
The child cries out when from the right breast the mother
     takes it away, in the very next moment to find in the
     left one its consolation.

XCVI

When I go from hence let this be my parting word, that
   what I have seen is unsurpassable.
I have tasted of the hidden honey of this lotus that expands
   on the ocean of light, and thus am I blessed—let this be
   my parting word.
In this playhouse of infinite forms I have had my play and
   here have I caught sight of him that is formless.
My whole body and my limbs have thrilled with his touch
   who is beyond touch; and if the end comes here, let it
   come—let this be my parting word.

XCVII

When my play was with thee I never questioned who thou
wert. I knew nor shyness nor fear, my life was boisterous.

In the early morning thou wouldst call me from my sleep
like my own comrade and lead me running from glade
to glade.

On those days I never cared to know the meaning of songs
thou sangest to me. Only my voice took up the tunes,
and my heart danced in their cadence.

Now, when the playtime is over, what is this sudden sight
that is come upon me? The world with eyes bent upon
thy feet stands in awe with all its silent stars.

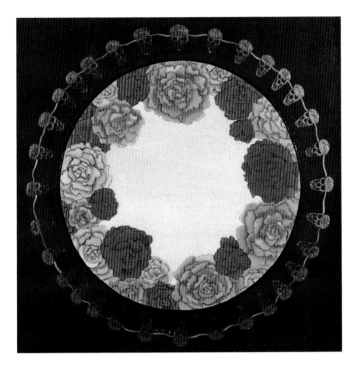

XCVIII

I will deck thee with trophies, garlands of my defeat.
    It is never in my power to escape unconquered.
I surely know my pride will go to the wall, my life will burst
    its bonds in exceeding pain, and my empty heart will
    sob out in music like a hollow reed, and the stone will
    melt in tears.
I surely know the hundred petals of a lotus will not remain
    closed forever and the secret recess of its honey will
    be bared.
From the blue sky an eye shall gaze upon me and summon
    me in silence. Nothing will be left for me, nothing
    whatever, and utter death shall I receive at thy feet.

XCIX

When I give up the helm I know that the time has come for
    thee to take it. What there is to do will be instantly
    done. Vain is this struggle.
Then take away your hands and silently put up with your
    defeat, my heart, and think it your good fortune to sit
    perfectly still where you are placed.
These my lamps are blown out at every little puff of wind,
    and trying to light them I forget all else again and again.
But I shall be wise this time and wait in the dark, spreading
    my mat on the floor; and whenever it is thy pleasure,
    my lord, come silently and take thy seat here.

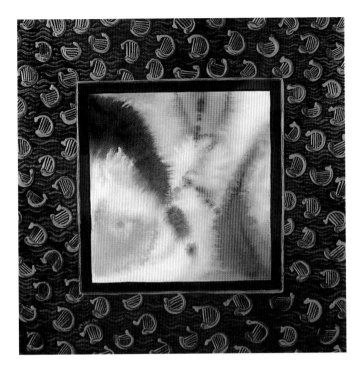

C

I dive down into the depth of the ocean of forms, hoping to
gain the perfect pearl of the formless.
No more sailing from harbour to harbour with this my
weather-beaten boat. The days are long passed when
my sport was to be tossed on waves.
And now I am eager to die into the deathless.
Into the audience hall by the fathomless abyss where swells
up the music of toneless strings I shall take this harp
of my life.
I shall tune it to the notes of forever, and when it has sobbed
out its last utterance, lay down my silent harp at the
feet of the silent.

CI

Ever in my life have I sought thee with my songs. It was they
who led me from door to door, and with them have I
felt about me, searching and touching my world.

It was my songs that taught me all the lessons I ever learnt;
they showed me secret paths, they brought before my
sight many a star on the horizon of my heart.

They guided me all the day long to the mysteries of the
country of pleasure and pain, and, at last, to what palace
gate have the brought me in the evening at the end of
my journey?

CII

I boasted among men that I had known you. They see your
    pictures in all works of mine. They come and ask me,
    "Who is he?" I know not how to answer them. I say,
    "Indeed, I cannot tell." They blame me and they go away
    in scorn. And you sit there smiling.
I put my tales of you into lasting songs. The secret gushes
    out from my heart. They come and ask me, "Tell me all
    your meanings." I know not how to answer them. I say,
    "Ah, who knows what they mean!" They smile and go
    away in utter scorn. And you sit there smiling.

CIII

In one salutation to thee, my God, let all my senses spread
    out and touch this world at thy feet.
Like a rain-cloud of July hung low with its burden of unshed
    showers let all my mind bend down at thy door in one
    salutation to thee.
Let all my songs gather together their diverse strains into
    a single current and flow to a sea of silence in one
    salutation to thee.
Like a flock of homesick cranes flying night and day back to
    their mountain nests let all my life take its voyage to
    its eternal home in one salutation to thee.

RECOMMENDED READING

Of the many biographies written on Tagore, one of the most balanced and informative is generally considered to be:

Rabindranath Tagore: The Myriad-Minded Man, Krishna Dutta and Andrew Robinson. New Delhi: Rupa & Co., 1997.

A broad sampling of the author's poems, plays, letters, essays, short stories and other writings is offered in:

A Tagore Reader, edited by Amiya Chakravarty. Boston: Beacon Press, 1966.

The translations of Tagore by William Radice are considered to be among the best. Interestingly, some Bengalis consider Radice's translations to be superior to Tagore's English translations of his own work.

Selected Short Stories, Rabindranath Tagore, translated by William Radice. London: Penguin Books, 1994.

Selected Poems, Rabindranath Tagore, translated by William Radice. London: Penguin Books, 1994.

For readers simply desiring to immerse themselves in Tagore for the foreseeable future, the following three large-format volumes contain over 2500 pages of Tagore's writings in English. Yet this is but a small fraction of his writings in Bengali—as Indian friends have commented, "If you truly wish to read and understand Tagore, learn Bengali."

The English Writings of Rabindranath Tagore. Volume One: Poems, edited by Sisir Kumar Das (New Delhi: Sahitya Akademi, 1994)

The English Writings of Rabindranath Tagore. Volume Two: Plays, Stories, and Essays, edited by Sisir Kumar Das. New Delhi: Sahitya Akademi, 1996.

The English Writings of Rabindranath Tagore. Volume Three: A Miscellany, edited by Sisir Kumar Das. New Delhi: Sahitya Akademi, 1996.

FLOATING WORLD EDITIONS and MAPIN BOOKS
publish works that contribute to a deeper understanding of
Asian cultures. Editorial supervision: Ray Furse. Book and
cover design: Liz Trovato. Production supervision: Bill Rose.
Printing and binding: Oceanic Graphics, Inc. The typefaces used
are Schneidler and Spectrum.